A BUREAUCRAT'S LOOK

AT GOVERNANCE

Welles Matias de Abreu

2020

Abreu, Welles Matias de
    A Bureaucrat's look at Governance
/ Welles Matias de Abreu. – Brasília, DF. 2020.
46 p.

    1. Brazil. 2. Governance. 3. Public Service.
4. State. 5. Society.

"Homo sapiens rules the world because it is the only animal that can believe in things that exist purely in its own imagination"

Yuval Noah Harari,

In Sapiens – A Brief History of Humankind (2014)

SUMMARY

1. CONSIDERATIONS ON THE BUREAUCRAT

At the height of the waterfall season in Brazil's central plateau in 2020, I am cooped up at home because of the COVID quarantine. This is the new normal in the pandemic, but it has the advantage of allowing some reflections on life. So, I (from now on called Bureaucrat – as one of Brazil's civil servants – am spending my days in front of the computer, working and studying. It is in this tedious setting that I turned to some things that I always thought about doing, but never before had time.

In this context, I decided to write a trilogy of personal vignettes. Recently, I read the book *In Sapiens – A Brief History of Humankind*[1], published in 2014, in which the author Yuval Harari emphasizes the importance of stories passed down through the generations to support the formation of humanity. So, this encouraged me to start writing about my experience in public governance.

I have been an eyewitness to several governmental changes that have promoted the institutionalization of governance in the public sector. Therefore, I believe it is timely to recount these historic changes. Governance, in this context, refers to public administration theory, which has components related to strategy, control, and leadership and a focus on cooperative and democratic actions.

The choice of the chronicle style was based on my intention to convey my personal perceptions on the topic. This means that I do not have the pretension of recounting the absolute veracity of the facts. I humbly position myself as an eternal apprentice. On this point, my perceptions are the result of my life experience, that is, they do not start only when I joined the public service. Instead, they date to my early childhood.

In December 1975, my mother started her contractions for my birth in a small town in the state of Minas Gerais, with fewer than four thousand inhabitants. When she was traveling by car with my father to a hospital in a larger city, they experienced three incidents: two tire punctures and traffic jam caused by a landslide on the precarious road in the region. These were difficult times, but very well lived. The tales of strong love and overcoming challenges can indicate the origins of a life full of happiness and adventure.

Since infancy, I was aware of the social differences that rein in Brazil. My parents are a good example of this. My mother comes from a well-heeled family, while my father was born in poverty. My father started working at the age of nine carrying sand

and planting pumpkins, while my mother studied at the best boarding school in the region.

While on vacation in my hometown, it was even comical how people greeted me. The humblest people called me Big Matias' son (my father's surname), while the upper class people called me the grandson of Joseph (my mother's father). This reflects the contrasts resulting from inequalities that led me to choose to serve my country and carry out scientific research to help, in some way, to reduce them.

In the late 1970s, my father – seeking better conditions for his family and tired of the political intrigues of our small hometown – went looking for a new occupation in the public sector. His fate was uncertain, but his desire was fulfilled by passing the public exam, so we moved to the nation's new capital. This completely changed our future. In Brasília, we had access to good living conditions: health care; education; safety; and the newest technologies.

My childhood was full of pleasant moments and great family atmosphere for learning. My mother, an elementary school teacher and dedicated housewife offered me all the care and education needed. But in her mind I just wanted to play, pass my time with friends in the streets and only study by force. On the other hand, I did not perform poorly at school, nor did I stand out for scholarship. And from that period that lingers fondly in my memory, a dear teacher said something that marked me for the rest of my life: "boy, you can become a civil servant and help the government make the best decisions for our beloved country."

After a long time, of fear and distress of how that urging could become reality, my heart lightened when my PhD faculty advisor told me that "a significant contribution does not necessarily have to be big." Instead, a set of small contributions can generate a much larger result than just a big one. Anyway, then

I discovered myself as a being who could advance despite my limitations, and fulfill that prophesy of my dear teacher.

I was born during the military dictatorship. In my adolescence, I was a big fan of Brazilian rock bands during the early 1980s, whose songs contained strong criticism of the dictatorship. I grew up with a pro-democracy feeling. And I experienced the transition from dictatorship to democracy in the 1980s. For me, the transition became established when censorship ended. Since then, I have noticed that democracy comes at a cost. I believe that it is better to live in a democracy with exaggerations than without it. While democracy can be messy, it is better than any other form of government. It is in the institutional checks and balances that we achieve dialogue and collective growth. It is in cooperation that we take advantage of the synergies of our efforts and guarantee our freedom.

I earned bachelor's degrees in both administration and agronomy, the first at the age of 21. And at 22, I passed the public exam to work as a civil servant for the Federal Budget Secretariat. Then I obtained my agronomy degree at 23. It was at that time that the short vignette trilogy that I write here began. It is about me, Bureaucrat, and the implementation of Governance in Brazil. I hope you enjoy it! These stories are in the next three chapters and mainly reflect the periods of the administrations of presidents Fernando Henrique Cardoso (FHC), Luiz Inácio Lula da Silva (Lula) and Dilma Rousscff (Dilma). They, heads of state, are called by me Leviathans, in reference to the metaphorical figure of the philosopher Hobbes.

2. THE CHALLENGE OF MANAGERIALISM

When listening to the sad song of thrush on a bright morning in June 1998, a paradox was manifested in feelings of cold in the hands and warmth in the heart. I, Bureaucrat, assumed that day the duty to serve the State and Brazilian Society! Until that point, a lot of water had passed under the bridge.

In 1992, amid the backlash against corruption in government, I was among the protesters called "painted faces," describing the yellow and green stripes on our faces as a way to highlight our patriotism and the feeling of revolt against official corruption. For me, all that was new, including the beginning of my antagonism with the head of state, a figure in my mind equated with the Leviathan, due to his government's being the pivot of the so-called "budget dwarfs" scandal (referring to the fact that the ringleaders were congressional backbenchers, or legislative small fry).

That antagonism, expressed between the cross and the sword, or rather, between the State and Society, moved me at that moment. The impeachment (and eventual resignation) of President Collor, involving the diversion of resources through pork barrel budget riders based on arrangements between the executive and legislative branches, prompted me to study the public budget. Then, the long-sought currency stability achieved by the "Real Plan" in 1994, was another strong motivator to act in the public budget field.

People, especially the poor without access to bank accounts, no longer needed to run to the supermarket to buy everything for the month due to erosion of their pay by monthly inflation as high as

40%, or wait in long lines to buy items pending price hikes. Families could plan trips, and the madness ended of buying dollars in the black market to guarantee purchasing power. All these represented a huge change for my generation. But it had a price, in the guise of a high interest rate.

In this context, becoming a federal budget analyst to help in this stabilization process was just a matter of time in my mind. So, after joining, I went through four long months of brainwashing at a government school where the students were challenged to work for efficiency gains. All this, under the backdrop of management reform, was part of the attempt to overcome more than 20 years of delay compared to countries like England. After that period, my feeling was that I knew practically nothing about how to collaborate in such a competitive environment.

Despite all the natural excitement of starting a new stage in my life, I felt like a grain of sand on a beach. Imagine, at the age of 22, thinking you could change the world, and suddenly discovering that the world was a big iron cage. Even if I applied everything I knew, I could do little. To my relief, a level-headed co-worker soon advised me that in just two years he would understand something. What a comfort!

Another point clearly demonstrating the prison of the state bureaucracy happened in the first month of work, when another colleague mentioned the dictum that "to order is for those who have power; to submit is for those who have good sense." Surprisingly, a few months later, my files saved on a network storage drive were deleted. The message was clear to me. Where the order came from did not matter to me...

My biggest irritation was with the way greater efficiency was demanded. Simply doing more with less is no big deal. But the presence of outdated equipment, slow decisions from on high, and a high level of bureaucracy to make priority resources available, hampered everything. Friend of the boss had technological resources available, so they were more "competitive", with no basis in a managerial model.

However, none of this compares with the agony of when I met Leviathan in 1999! Now, in another guise, the Head of State was under suspicion in the context of the "BNDES phone tap" scandal, when illegal phone taps raised doubts about the legality of the auction of the telecom companies spun off from the Telebrás system. Although the evidence was collected illegally, the evident corruption rocked the government again. Sad for Society. This was terrible for my convictions...

But not everything about this episode was tragic. After a long and exhaustive work focused on managerial reform of the budgetary process, in 2000 Brazil had a new framework for fiscal management and a new program design. I proudly witnessed this movement first hand, which resulted in greater accountability, transparency and management for results in public finance.

Accountability transfers the burden of the failure of public decisions to the manager who makes them. This is, for instance, a key point in the Fiscal Responsibility Law of 2000 (LRF/2000), which played the key role in the impeachment of President Dilma Rousseff in 2015 based on her violation of that law. Furthermore, Decree 2829/1998, brought the figure of public manager, responsible for monitoring the results of government programs.

Transparency was already based to some extent on the definition of budget classifiers. The requirement for publication of official acts also acts as a guarantee of public access to budgetary actions. The innovation here was the access to spending execution data in a clear and timely manner, also by virtue of the LRF/2000. So, the premise, or the rule, is transparency. In this context, secrecy is the exception.

Later, the Information Access Law (LAI/2011) expanded this rule to other public service processes.

The introduction of new contractual instruments allowed more flexibility in contracting services by governmental entities, with focus on results-based management and lower costs. Such instruments were inspired by international experiences – for instance, the New Zealand management reform – and promoted the implementation of regulatory agencies and the decentralization of services to nongovernmental organizations, in an attempt, albeit embryonic, to enable more public oversight of public officials. In the coming years, the strengthening of the relationship between State and society will be urgent.

Against the backdrop of these advances, I learned to be resilient... So, I had the perception that a war is won by battles, where some battles could be lost, but knowing how to take advantage of victories is a crucial strategy.

In December 2000, when Robert and Janet Denhardt published the article "The new public service: serving instead of driving[2]," I felt great. Their conclusion was that the State should encourage the participation of society in government decisions, by strengthening public discourse and interest, so that democratic values become the basis for a new way of governing, called Governance. The ember of hope was kindled!

3. THE RENDEZVOUS WITH GOVERNANCE

It was January 2003, and I, Bureaucrat, found myself again in the midst of paradoxes. On the one hand was euphoria over my wedding preparations; on the other, doubts about what would come with the assumption of a new President. His profile at that moment conveyed peace and love. But he had a background of strident union radicalism. At that time, I was taking on an important position in a ministry and my wife was fired from her job. Moments of great joy and apprehension.

At the age of 27 and with five years of experience in the public service, I was more prepared. I was no longer that person who wanted to change the world. I already had a good perception of what was around me and what shaped me. I was aware that in an office in Brasilia, one could not have the full perception of a people, a territory or the nation. My specific function was to contribute to the functioning of the State. However, I still worried about how to contribute effectively to society. So, I lived one day at a time, from a humble person's perspective, limited in resources and reasoning, but eager to do the best for my country!

Big changes came with the institutionalization of new paradigms. A new era was beginning, where Leviathan's speech seemed to sound like music to the poor and to those who defend public service. Soon, my wife started working for the postal service. And, my governmental perception changed. The creation of several public policy councils with social participation; the fight against hunger and extreme poverty; and the search for transparency would accompany the fight against corruption. Would it really be a rendezvous between the State and society? Let us see...

Within a few months, already confident of my bureaucratic assignments related to the public budget in my new job, I received a call. In five minutes, I was in the minister's office along with his deputy. On the way, my memories were of the paternal sayings that a good technician is one who does not mix with politicians. But a politician was my boss. And, also, he was the representative of the State to society. Anyway, I did not know that, when I entered his office, that I would have an experience to last a lifetime. After two minutes, a singular question arose: "Friend, how did my predecessors pilfer from this ministry?" My quick reply was: "I have no idea because I wasn't here before." Then, the minister's one-sided farewell was: "Thank you, my boy, we're done now."

Days later, I witnessed an extremely level-headed (today my friend) who worked with government contracts, handing in his resignation. At the same time, the deputy minister, who invited me to work at the ministry, was fired. This cast doubt in my mind over whether that question was an attempt to understand the corruption process in order to curb it or to continue plundering the public coffers. Well, from then on, my mission was just to finish the coordination of the ministry's budget process for the following year.

There were moments of anguish. Two months passed like two years. I participated in meetings that questioned the reason for my performance as a faithful guardian to respect the ministry's financial limits, but this did not divert me on iota from my responsibility, knowing the consequences of violating the LRF/2000. I had a clear notion that my time was really ending in that posting, because I broke, in the certainty of having done the right thing, the well-known public service mantra "to order is for those who have power; to submit is for those who have good sense."

Thus, in 2005, a huge scandal arose involving politicians of the president's party (Workers Party). The party's treasurer and the presidential chief of staff were accused (and later found guilty) of orchestrating a scheme that paid monthly allowances to members of Congress (hence called the "big allowance" scheme) in return for favorable votes, with the money coming from padding the advertising budgets of State-controlled companies. So, I came across an invigorated Leviathan who illegally used his State power to ride roughshod over the representative power of society.

What this Leviathan gave with one hand, he took back with the other. Corruption still remained entrenched in Brazil, hitting the core of government again. In 2006, the minister of finance resigned after complaints about receiving bribes when he was a mayor.

Unfortunately, later the State's approach to contractors exposed yet another perverse face of government corruption, which eventually resulted in the first arrest of a Leviathan in Brazil. Public spending, mostly on works performed by large construction companies, exploded, motivated mainly by the professed need for anti-cyclical fiscal policy in reaction to the international crisis of 2008.

During that period, I had the opportunity to work in two regulatory agencies, where management by results impressed me. It was a new world for me, with proximity to society, when I witnessed public hearings and consultations that involved delivering services to society. I saw, with my "own eyes," the occurrence of meetings of public agents broadcast in real-time by the media. All this awoke my thirst to cooperate with the promotion of increased transparency and social participation.

In search of peace, due to the imminent birth of my first child in 2007, I decided to return to the place where my professional career started, the Federal Budget Secretariat, or better, my home. It was another time. There was a thriving environment of ideas and events. I had the opportunity to develop my master's thesis in theory and practice. Instruments for the emancipation of society in the budget process were implemented. Brazil's international leadership was a reality. We were present at forums of the Inter-American Development Bank, the Global Initiative for Fiscal Transparency and the Government Opening Partnership.

At this unique moment, I met Governance. I saw, breathed, and embraced the actions that promoted the emancipation of society, especially regarding the budget process. Implementation of actions to promote transparency and social participation in the budget process were recognized for the consequent improvements in Brazil in the ranking of countries in the Open Budget Indicator produced by the International Budget Partnership. Being resilient is not easy, but it is worthwhile when you have a purpose based on solid pillars. And, one of these pillars was the work of Osborne in 2006, called "The new public governance?[3]," which ratified the new era in public administration with stress on cooperation of all stakeholders. I felt even more secure on the path I was taking!

4. SEARCHING FOR GOOD GOVERNANCE

The skin wrinkles, pain in the back and joints and the various sudden acute illnesses previously not suffered were a sign for me, Bureaucrat, of the arrival of maturity. The year 2011 was a very interesting transition moment in my personal life. The arrival of my second child marked my perception.

The same light that warmed me in the mornings is the same light that renews life in the Cerrado (Savanna) after the spring rains. I was in control of my life. I guided myself in full awareness. More hits, fewer misses. So, if changing the world was not possible, changing my attitude in search of improvements was fully feasible and desirable.

From that moment on, I had the opportunity to make several international trips, not only to debate and present professional results, but also to expose my ideas and academic findings. I sometimes had been in the premises of international organizations – such as the World Bank, Inter-American Development and International Monetary Fund – which I never imagined could contribute to the results of my work. Now it crossed my mind that I might be able to enter their headquarters in the capital of the United States.

As a result of Brazil's effort, in 2012 the United Nations adopted, in 2012 a Resolution encouraging its member countries to promote actions for transparency, participation and accountability, as well as to reward the initiative of the Inter-Council Forum in 2014.

The world was already under a new order whose spirit came from Governance. And in Brazil this was no different, even with the change of the presidency, the continuation of the same party in power prompted the expectation for us to continue advancing in this direction. For example, the enactment of the Information Access Law (LAI/2011) was a Governance triumph. Cooperation was the watchword (and it still sounds like music today).

New expressions come into fashion to support the delivery of public products and services. Cowork, codesign and coparticipation are some examples of this institutionalization of processes never seen with such strength. A sign of this was the virtuous growth of a new transportation network company through "ride hailing" that uses the concept of cooperation as the basis of its operations, becoming in less than a decade one of the largest in the world in this sector.

Unfortunately, in 2011, President Dilma Rousseff started to sink in the opinion polls after the announcements of several ministerial changes due to suspicions of wrongdoing. The following year, I heard on the radio about the arrest of many bigwigs of the

Workers Party due to the crimes arising from the "Big Allowance" scandal. Finally, and even bigger scandal hit in 2014 with the establishment of "Operação Lava Jato" ("Operation Car Wash"), triggering a sequence of events that deeply affected the nation.

At that time, I had the clear perception that although the change of head of state had occurred. In practice, the previous Leviathan (Lula) remained in charge. Mismanagement took over the State. The consequent lack of control over public accounts generated questionable acts that led to the possibility of President Rousseff being held responsible.

In this difficult moment, the trigger for the opening of an impeachment process came from a set of factors that led to a "perfect storm." Popular movements motivated by the so-called Arab Spring, which started in Tunisia, spread to several countries the demand for better government results, such as the reduction of corruption. Greater transparency allowed access to data on budgetary decisions, highlighting fiscal shenanigans whereby budget holes were filled by obtaining loans from state-controlled banks in violation of the Fiscal Responsibility Law. The advance of the "Car Wash" investigations generated huge dissatisfaction among lawmakers and the public with the president, aggravated by a sluggish economy the sank into recession. All of this ignited the fuse for the materialization of the impeachment of Dilma Rousseff.

After large street protests, pan-beating and an acrimonious process in Congress, in 2016 the president was impeached and her vice president, Michel Temer, took over. At the time I was on leave to devote full time to my scientific research on Governance. Although very busy at that time, my mind kept thinking about what this new government would be like. And it was not for nothing, as the new president almost immediately came under suspicion of involvement in corruption, including public disclosure of a recording of a secret meeting between him and the owner of a large meat packing company, revealing high-level bribery for favorable administrative rulings. The corruption seemed endless.

At that time, although certain that advances in Governance were already consolidated, I posed a question to myself: When will the results of Governance become effective? For example, when would the perception of corruption improve in Brazil?

In 2017, after an invitation from a friend, I returned to work in government activities, now in a new area of a ministry created to implement Governance resource projects related to international cooperation. Oops, remember, cooperation is a premise for good Governance. With the confidence acquired by professional maturity and academic discernment, it was an experience full of uncertainties due to the complex theme and the small organizational structure available. But the results came and so did the recognition. Soon he was acting as an assistant to the deputy minister. I noticed that Governance had gone from being a theoretical proposal to a practical and viable reality from different perspectives.

It has no resilience without recognition. Even if internal, feeling rewarded is essential to insist on doing right. In 2017, a scientific work produced during my PhD studies on Governance was received an award at the annual meeting of the Brazilian Administration Association. That achievement, in the face of my doubt (which bothered me and continues to bother me), prodded me to continue my journey of searching for more enlightenment on this theme.

Finally, 2019 was marked by the publication of the book by Acemoglu and Robinson called *The Narrow Corridor: States, Societies, and the Fate of Liberty* [4], which presents Leviathan from the perspective of the powers of the State and society.

This filled me with the expectation of obtaining a valid explanation of how the results of Governance can become effective.

5. PERSPECTIVES ON GOVERNANCE

Resilience. This is undoubtedly the word that has moved me over the past 20 years. Rewinding is not an option. Some battles may have even been in vain. But final victory will come with time. So, I learned by watching the advances of Governance. Even though I cannot change the world on my own, I see that it is the set of small initiatives carried out by people in the public sector in a collaborative manner that has led to the greatest results of Governance achieved to date. For this, technology tools are essential!

It was in this spirit that the advances in Governance occurred in Brazil. With leadership initiatives in the ministries and the core government; with strategies seeking integration between ministerial and government plans; with control focused on society and transparency with a view to promoting accountability of the government to the governed. However, putting this model into practice remains a challenge.

After the Governance institutions are consolidated, the possibility of regression is doubtful. But you cannot hesitate! Authoritarian and corrupt winds coming from Leviathan are always knocking on the door of our young democracy, threatening, for instance, the recent gains from social participation. And democratic institutions are the basis for the still necessary full implementation of Governance.

I found evidence that demonstrates that social development comes through improving Governance results, available in my thesis "Unlocking the government door[5]." So, Governance is a valid and opportune way to reduce poverty, and consequently Brazil's social inequalities. And encouraging the emergence of collaborative stakeholders is assuredly the best way to achieve gains in social development.

Therefore, continuing to contribute to the implementation of Governance actions is essential, seeking new evidence on the topic, namely: Why have there been no improvements in the perception of corruption despite the greater transparency and social participation? How will Leviathan react over time based on democratic variables? What moderation does transparency have with the perception of corruption in countries with or without democracy? These are just a few issues that still stir me up...

REFERENCES

1. HARARI, Yuval N. **Sapiens: A brief history of humankind**. Random House, 2014.

2. DENHARDT, Robert B.; DENHARDT, Janet Vinzant. The new public service: Serving rather than steering. **Public administration review**, v. 60, n. 6, p. 549-559, 2000.

3. OSBORNE, Stephen P. The new public governance? **Public management review**. v. 8, n. 3, p. 377-87, 2006.

4. ACEMOGLU, Daron; ROBINSON, James A. **The narrow corridor: States, societies, and the fate of liberty**. Penguin Press, 2019.

5. ABREU, Welles M. **Unlocking the government door to society: how does open budgeting relate to social development?** Universidade de Brasília, 2017.

PHRASES ABOUT THE AUTHOR

"With a strategic vision and clear Governance concepts, it drafted norms and the main legal instruments that provided transparency and provided accountability for international projects"

Romeu Mendes do Carmo,
Ex Vice Ministry of Environment

"His performance has always sought to add value to the actions of the bodies where he worked, always with a focus on improving spending and its results on society"

Eliomar Wesley Ayres da Fonseca Rios,
Ex Vice Secretary of the Brazilian Budget Secretariat

THE AUTHOR

Welles Matias de Abreu

Brazilian federal public servant in the position of Planning and Budget Analyst at the Federal Budget Secretariat (since 1998). PhD (2017) and Master (2011) in Administration from the University of Brasília, specialist in Public Management (2009) from the Escola Nacional de Administração Pública, and in Planning, Budget and Public Management (2002) from Fundação Getúlio Vargas, graduated in Agronomic Engineering (1999) by the Universidade of Brasília, and in Administration (1997) by the Centro Universitário do Distrito Federal.

He has professional experience focused on public budgeting, government planning, strategic management, organizational modernization, people management, institutional development, combating corruption and money laundering, information systems management, fiscal transparency, external resource management, engagement of civil society, and audit focused on risk management.

He has served as General Coordinator / Manager / Advisor for Planning, Budget, Finance and Accounting in Ministries related to public policies on Social Security, Social Assistance, Labor, Environment, Electricity and Federal Budget, as well as Director of External Resources within the scope International Cooperation in the Environment (more than 80 supervised projects), Planning and Audit Monitoring Coordinator of the National Water Agency.

CV: http://lattes.cnpq.br/4517474555485897

Note: The Images in this Book must be credited to the Author.

"Governance is a valid and opportune way to reduce poverty"

Welles Matias de Abreu

A BUREAUCRAT'S LOOK

AT GOVERNANCE